Ryan Howland Musical Awakening

Ryan Howland

authorHOUSE®

AuthorHouse™
1663 Liberty Drive
Bloomington, IN 47403
www.authorhouse.com
Phone: 1 (800) 839-8640

Published by AuthorHouse 10/03/2016

ISBN: 978-1-5246-4274-7 (sc)
ISBN: 978-1-5246-4273-0 (e)

Print information available on the last page.

ABOUT THE AUTHOR

RYAN HOWLAND IS a Taiwanese-Canadian violinist born in Victoria BC, Canada. At just 17 years old, he has already performed numerous concerts all across the globe in Canada, Taiwan, Germany, England, France and Switzerland. He has also won prizes in many competitions such as 1st prize in the International Grand Prize Virtuoso Music Competition in London and 1st prize in the BC Performing Arts Festival in Canada. Ryan Howland's ultimate goal is to become a world renowned violin virtuoso, performing all over the world. His new enthusiasm for writing books is meant to help spread the word of his incredible stories and experiences as well as the countless hardships and setbacks he has overcome while pursuing music to the highest level.

DEDICATED TO:

My Supporters,
Uncle Tsai
Marcel B.
Dr. Loschen
Hans E.
Dirk M.
Tania M.

My Teachers,
Michael van der Sloot
Maurizio Sciarretta
Rudolf Koelman
Viktor Tretyakov

and many more...

TABLE OF CONTENTS

PROLOGUE

MY MIND WAS etched with the spectacular image of Maxim Vengerov's poignant performance of the Franck Sonata at the Verbier Festival in Switzerland. The world famous violinist swayed to and fro in such a way that transported the audience into the realm of music. I was awestruck by his sheer genius. The seemingly dull black music notes came to life and danced around the stage under the commandment of Vengerov's bow. At age 14, I wanted to be on the same stage beside him. The way the melodies and harmonies blended together made my hair stand on end. I was moved like never before. My mother, brother and I left with a changed perspective. This was the work of one of the most celebrated musicians in the world. - I thought.

After the concert, people were swarming backstage to greet the maestro. I also wanted to see him and maybe ask for a photo, but it was too much for me at the time. I was just a shy boy who lacked confidence. I went back to the apartment with my mother and brother, empty handed and drought in disappointment. The truth was, I did want to meet Maxim Vengerov, but just didn't have enough self-esteem. My mother saw the regret on my face then quickly slipped outside while muttering,

"I'll be back."

Although it was pouring rain outside, my mother proceeded to walk all the way back to the concert venue to get Vengerov's autograph. The concert itself was already long over, but that didn't faze her. She was just following her instincts and wanted to cheer me up. Luckily, Maxim Vengerov was just about to leave the dressing room when she arrived, clothes soaked and shoes ruined from the rain. She had brought along with her my recent certificate from a masterclass with world renowned pedagogue Zakhar Bron, Maxim Vengerov's former teacher and she hastily asked him to sign it. A few moments later, the certificate had a huge autograph crossed through the middle with two words written below it. Some of the two biggest words that would soon change my life forever,

"Practice well!"

FOUNDATION

Certificate

Ryan Howland

has attended as an Active Participant at the

Violin Master Class

INTRODUCTION

THE WILL TO sacrifice was a quality that I forced myself to realize as a child. To persevere in the toughest and most pressuring situations is an essential trait for any serious musician. This is especially true for the violinist, musician and artist that I strive to become. Ever since I came into the world of music, I have developed hand in hand with the violin and set forth a passionate and determined path towards my goals. What I aspire to achieve is something much greater than the norm. On top of the hard work and drive required, I will need to overcome all of my hardships and financial barriers in order to become a soloist at the top of the violin world. My vision is clear and I can see the future unraveling. My unwavering confidence will guide me in my pursuit.

This story portrays the early life and heart wrenching journey of young violinist, Ryan Howland, who is willing to sacrifice everything in order to achieve his goals – explained through his personal reflections and short stories.

CHAPTER

Shore

BEING OF MIXED race, I was raised and influenced by both western and eastern cultures. My mother was born in Taiwan and moved to Canada as a student. Her own pursuit of her dreams lead her to begin a new life in Victoria BC, an island on the west coast of Canada. She herself was a hard working piano student, practicing up to 8 hours a day. However, that ceased when she married my Canadian father- the principle trombonist in the symphony. She then chose to direct her focus away from the piano and onto her family life. My brother, Ian Howland, was born 3 years before me, and my parents divorced when I was only 2 years old.

Because I grew up with my mother, I was raised more strictly in the traditional Chinese way and was given many more opportunities than the average child. I broadened my mind and skill set through various activities in both sports and the arts such as skating, swimming, soccer, tennis, karate, fishing, painting, piano and violin. I was also fortunate enough to be exposed to the wondrous occasions of opera and symphony concerts. As my father dedicated himself to the symphony for many years, he was able to get us free concert tickets.

Music was always flowing through my household. For as long as I can remember, I would wake up every day to the delicate sound of the piano. My mother was an extremely busy piano teacher, teaching both at the conservatory and at home, from early in the morning to late at night. Along with my brother, I became accustomed to the subtle sounds and vibrations of the music that was constantly being poured into my ears. Eventually, we were even able to memorize the many melodies of the standard piano repertoire. Although we did not know the names, we could distinguish by heart most of the famous piano works. It was always lively at home, as students would come in and out of the house every hour. I sometimes found it a lack of privacy, but it also gave me the opportunity to play and make friends with the students.

As a whole, my childhood was quite stable and relaxing. Growing up in a peaceful neighborhood in one of the most beautiful and seamless cities in the world shaped my early lifestyle. I never had any real problems nor serious difficulties. We had everything we needed: education, sports, friends and a nice small house. For a child, it was the perfect place to grow up; a clean environment with beautiful nature and playgrounds every few blocks. Our area was particularly attractive to wild animals that even passing deer would often stop by for naps in the backyard. Nowadays, with my newly gained insight on the world, I have realized just how lucky I was to have been born and raised in such a city. In the beginning, I was no different from an ordinary child. But thanks to the many opportunities I was given from an early age, I had a little bit more determination and potential than others.

As my mother was a single parent, we were by no means wealthy. Even though we were given so many unique opportunities, it was only possible thanks to my mother's determination and generosity to give us the best and least worry-some lives as she could.

Kayaking near my home city in Canada

CHAPTER

First Chore

M Y PARENTS WERE extremely busy while I was growing up. I spent a great deal of time just waiting around for my mother to finish teaching at the music conservatory as she was simply too busy to take care of my brother and I during her work. However, at the ripe age of 5, she finally decided on the perfect solution. As my mother was a very strong classical music lover, she decided to sign my brother and me up for music lessons. The chosen instruments were the piano and violin, for no particular reason. It could have easily been something like the clarinet or tuba, but I think my mother was a little bit fonder of the violin and piano. In a way, the violin came to me initially as a form of babysitting, which soon after turned into one of my most favorite hobbies. More importantly, my mother would no longer be worried that my brother and I would have nothing to do.

I had many teachers during the first few years of playing the violin, but I only played for fun and that was how my teachers treated me as well. At first, I had no preference with either the violin or piano. It was all just music to me and I enjoyed having so many possibilities beneath my fingertips. The first person who really brought me to love playing the violin was my teacher, Michael van der Sloot, whom I had met when I was 10 years old. He encouraged me to take the violin a little bit more seriously and helped me develop out of being a young boy and into a young adult. It was then that I decided to quit the piano and focus only on the violin as that was where my true passion laid. By the age of 10, I began practicing at least an hour per day. Before that, I played as little as 20 minutes per day. It still wasn't much, but it was a big improvement and the fact that I was taking it more seriously mattered the most. However, I still considered the violin as a mere hobby and nowhere near my top priorities.

By the age of 12 at 13, my two most favorite activities became playing the violin and tennis. Sometimes, I even took tennis more seriously than violin. As there were free tennis courts nearby our house, my brother and I used to walk over there to train every day. We would practice for hours and challenge each other in matches day after day to see who was better. Since he was older, he was always a little bit better than me which made me want to beat him even more. I played many tournaments, winning some and losing some. I was extremely competitive and always lusted for the thrill of being on court. Thanks to my life as a competitive tennis player, I gained an enormous amount of experience dealing with stress, anxiety and endurance that I use today in my violin performance. While on court, one has to face all kinds of emotional challenges alone: frustration, anger, willpower, relief and everything that a music performer must go through. As I got older, my mindset from playing tennis eventually poured into my field of music. Tennis became one of my many hobbies, and all of my determination and passion transferred to playing the violin. In the end, all of the skills I acquired from my many activities went into developing myself as a human being, and moreover enhancing my desire to make music.

10 year old Ryan taking home the bronze
medal from a tennis tournament

CHAPTER  3

All for Music

FOR AS LONG as I can remember, I have always loved performing music for others and I always look for different opportunities to express myself. In elementary school, I would often bring my violin to school to show my teachers and classmates. I was mostly a shy boy, but I showed my true colors through the violin. I was a show off. After school, I would rush outside and whip out my violin and just start playing. I always tried to be the first one outside so that everyone would have plenty of time to hear me. I never felt a shred of doubt in what I was doing; I was just so fond of sharing my unique talent with others, even if I was only able to play a few simple pieces from the Suzuki Method. As a boy, my favorite part about performing was the praise and compliments that my friends would give me after each piece. They would even give me ridiculous nicknames like Mozart or call me a robot, even though I surely did not compare to the real genius of Mozart. I never admitted it, but I loved being the center of attention and acting like it's no big deal when clearly, everyone was impressed.

During my third year of elementary school, I was 9 years old and was eagerly looking forward to showing off my violin skills in the upcoming school talent show. Less than one month prior to the event, I got into an accident in gym class and resultantly broke my left arm. The experience is still fresh in my memory and I still remember the painfully haunting feeling I felt that day.

I was lying face down on a mattress surrounded by my classmates when one of them accidentally fell on my arm. I didn't have any time to react as I had looked over my shoulder just milliseconds before my friend's elbow made complete contact with the side of my left forearm. The agonizing pain came coursing through only a few moments later. I was confused and didn't know exactly what had happened; I just wanted to get out of there as soon as possible. Quickly and cautiously, I grabbed my backpack and snuck out of the school without anybody noticing. The last thing I wanted was to ruin the mood by making a dramatic scene in front of everybody and I also didn't want my classmate to feel guilty. Instead, I decided to leave myself to writhe alone while my friends continued playing without me.

It was the end of the school day as I sat outside to wait for my mother, who didn't yet know of my injury, to come and take me home- although a detour to the hospital first awaited me. I recall a humorous moment while I was sitting outside, a senior lady beside me noticed that I was clutching my arm uncomfortably.

"Are you cold?" She asked.

"No, my arm just hurts," I replied with a blatantly sarcastic tone.

I had to wear a cast covering everything from my elbow and up for a month. My wrist was locked in place and I could only wriggle the tips of my fingers ever so slightly. My violin teacher at the time said that it would be impossible to play the violin in the talent show. I could only practice a few simple bowing exercises with my right hand for the whole duration of my recovery. I was so excited to perform the violin for my peers, only to have that chance taken away from me in the blink of an eye, it was a huge disappointment. However, even without the violin, I still wanted to perform music and I was not going to let a measly broken arm prevent me from doing so. After all, I still had one last option. There was no way I would play the violin for the talent show, but after some experiments, I decided

I would be able to play the piano instead. Unlike on the violin, it was much easier to compensate for the left hand on the piano. Since my left fingers were not completely immobile, I simply used my right hand to play more of the left hand notes along with a few improvised tricks and the result was a success. The audience and my friends were so amazed that their praise of my bravery and talent didn't stop pouring in. Afterwards, I couldn't stop bragging about how I performed in the talent show with a broken arm!

Turning Point

ASIDE FROM PLAYING the violin, I considered myself to have been a pretty normal kid. I put a fair amount of work into my craft, but I still did not know just how far I wanted to take it. It was when I turned 14 that everything became clear as day. All it took was one life changing experience, one that made me realize my true dream of becoming a world famous violinist as well as the unbelievable amount of sacrifice and determination that would be required to do so. My eyes finally opened after meeting Professor Zakhar Bron in Zurich, Switzerland.

My mother is a constant volunteer at the Verbier Festival in Switzerland- one of the biggest and most famous music festivals in the world. Held in the beautiful setting of the Swiss Alps, many of the world's finest musicians are invited every year to perform there. As a volunteer, my mother could watch free concerts and masterclasses every day. One year, she had the opportunity to watch a student masterclass with world renowned violin pedagogue Zakhar Bron. I was about 10 years old when my mother first encountered him. After the class, she boldly approached him wondering about instruments and where to find the best violins. Luckily, professor Bron was in a good enough mood to introduce her to the violin luthier at the festival and they then took a taxi together to see him. My mother was a little bit naïve at the time; she wasn't actually interested in buying any instruments, nor did she have the money to do so, she was just curious and wanted to meet as many people as possible. What she didn't know was that she had just so happened to come across one of the biggest and most influential violin teachers in the world who had taught some of the world's best violinists like Vadim Repin and Maxim Vengerov. He was also the teacher who would eventually change my life. My mother waited several years until she thought I was good enough to apply for professor Bron's masterclass program in Zurich, Switzerland. When I was 14 years old, we decided to apply and miraculously, I was accepted.

I stayed by myself in a small apartment of a friend while my mother volunteered for the Verbier Festival at the same time. Because we did not have much money to spend, I brought along from Canada 8 cans of chicken and beef soup to eat for the whole week. I knew how expensive it would be in Switzerland; I needed to reduce the costs as much as possible. During the entire stay, I spent only 5 Swiss Francs on food and necessities. Everything else was already prepared. It took a lot of work and sacrifice just for the one week of lessons, but it was definitely worth it, as this would be one of the biggest turning points in my young career as a violinist.

And so came the first day of the masterclass. I was sitting in the audience with all the other participants and spectators, waiting for professor Bron to arrive and teach the first lesson. He casually walked in half an hour late, made a brief introduction and began his class.

Astonished, was my first impression of professor Bron's teaching style. He was attentive, straight to the point and extremely picky about the smallest of details. I couldn't believe how much he cared about every little thing, and his great knowledge of music was extraordinary. As for the level of playing, it was first-rate; I was dumbfounded. The skill level of his students was so unbelievable high that it was overwhelming for the young and inexperienced boy that I was; I felt like the smallest fish in the ocean. I had still not yet devoted myself to playing the violin seriously and I only practiced a maximum of two hours per day at the time. I soon realized the naïveté of my lack of commitment as I was forced to face the truth. My first lesson with professor Bron came quickly and went by just as quickly.

My lesson was scheduled last for the day. Professor Bron seemed tired and impatient. I nervously went up on stage to begin my performance of "Scherzo Tarantella" by the Polish composer Henryk Wieniawsky. To put it simply, it was not my best impression. I immediately felt intimidated by the daunting gaze of professor Bron. I tried to remember my mother's words from our phone call the previous day, telling me to stay calm. She tried to convince me of how professor Bron was just a normal person and no one special away from the violin. But despite her efforts, it didn't get through to me. The pressure was too great for the shy "nobody" that I was and I didn't have enough confidence in my own skill. Growing up in a peaceful city with no real ambitions made me too laid back, the reality of violin slapped me hard in the face.

Finally, I began my unemotional performance, playing like a robot that was not programmed correctly to play in tune or in tempo. I blundered through passages, missed notes and produced a shallow sound. When I finished, I knew that nobody was going to be impressed. Professor Bron was usually energetic during lessons as I had observed previously with other students. However this time, he spoke harshly and reluctantly as if he didn't even want to teach an awful student like me. I was too young and inexperienced; professor Bron overpowered me. Twenty minutes into the lesson, he sat down and looked me right in the eye for a good few seconds of what seemed like hours. He then said one word, the single word that changed my life forever.

"Practice," he said.

And that was the end of the lesson.

In a lesson with professor Zakhar Bron in Switzerland

CHAPTER

Practice

IT TOOK A few months for professor Bron's advice to really sink in. I eventually realized that if I wanted to catch up to professor Bron's students, I would need to start practicing harder and better. I spent a lot of time just thinking about it before making my decision. At first, I didn't want to accept that I would have to sacrifice so many more hours every day to practice. The time I would usually spend going out, playing tennis, or just relaxing would disappear completely. Knowing all of this, I still wanted to do it. I had established a new goal and the freshly lit fire inside of me kept pushing me towards it.

I began with three hours per day and continued with that amount for several months. At the time, it was my limit. My muscles would wear out even with short breaks in between each hour. Sometimes, I would even feel sharp throbbing pains in my left forearm as I wasn't used to playing more a couple of hours per day.

Slowly yet carefully, I pushed it to four hours per day. Then five or six. It became easier and easier to endure as I progressed. It was like a game to me. "Could I focus through six hours of good practicing every day?"- was the question I asked myself before every practice session. Finally, when I was 15, I reached the big eight hour mark. I felt great. Eight hours of solid practicing every day -easy. Before long, practicing eight hours a day became so natural that my priorities and sense of values started to get mixed up in my head. You could say that I just went crazy. School became the least of my concerns. I temporarily stopped going as I thought it was useless and was not going to help me play more in tune. I stopped playing tennis as well. As much as I loved being on court, I was surprised at how quickly I lost interest in it. On the days that I didn't have time to practice exactly eight hours, I would get the most terrible feeling in my stomach that wouldn't go away until I made up for it the next day. Playing the violin became so important to me that I felt like the whole world would end if I didn't practice enough. I wanted to get better more than anything and prove to everybody that I was just as good as professor Bron's students.

My parents and friends were shocked by what I was doing. Most students have to have their parents tell them to practice, but I made the decision completely on my own. Of course, it wasn't easy, however it was absolutely necessary. For a whole year, my daily schedule looked something like this:

10:00 am - wake up and eat breakfast
11:00 am to 2:00 pm - practice
2:00 pm to 5:00 pm - eat lunch and go out
5:00 pm to 8:00 pm - practice
8:00 pm to 9:00 pm - break and eat dinner
9:00 pm to 11:00 pm - practice
12:00 am - sleep and repeat

I carefully observed my quick progress and could see results every week. The most inhuman part that I still have a hard time believing is that I was able to stay 100% focused throughout the whole eight hours of good practicing. To put "good practice" into perspective, that meant practicing slow scales, études, Paganini Caprices, and loads of other repertoire with a great concern for detail and clarity. I practiced slower and more carefully than anybody else, determined to catch up to my fellow peers. At the end of the day, I felt as if the world had been saved.

CHAPTER

First Prize

CONFIDENCE WAS EVIDENTLY one of the most important traits that I lacked as a young performer. Especially after my first experience with Professor Bron, my self-esteem was not exactly as high as others. I was still quite shy and was yet to recognize my own potential. Soon after beginning my strict practice regimen, I was selected to compete for the first time outside the comfort of my home city at a provincial level competition. I was given the opportunity to test my skills and insight of music against a huge stream of violinists my age.

At first glance, one might not realize just how beneficial music competitions can be. Music is not a sport, it is art, although the preparation and training is no different from that of an athlete. To keep one's body and mind as fit and ready as possible and to assure that everything is as perfect as can be, is quite the demanding task. As musicians, we always strive to be the best of ourselves and competitions present a golden opportunity to do just that. At age 15, I was ready to make my first step into the competition world, and more importantly, I would finally get to see if the long hours of practice were paying off or not.

Before I could attend the competition, there was one last problem we had to sort outside. Financially, we couldn't even afford the costs for one person to go alone. As ambition as I was, I wanted to make it happen no matter how difficult it would be. If I could improve even just little bit, it would be worth it. There was no way I would let this opportunity slip away just because we lacked the money. Along with my mother's encouragement, I decided to busk every day leading up to the competition to raise all of the necessary costs. It was a strenuous process that took weeks of only practicing at home then playing on the streets all day long. In my mind, I wanted to be on stage performing so badly, despite what it would take to get there. Finally, I had made enough to manage the trip.

Aside from the instrumental preparation itself, the process of traveling to the competition, finding the venues and dealing with pressure was an all-new experience for me. After arriving at the competition location, I met up with my accompanist and my teacher's wife. They were both kind enough to drive me back and forth from the hotel to the performance hall and even take me out to eat. I never realized just how important it was to have supportive people around, as things would have been much harder without them.

When the competition day came, I was confident and nervous at the same time. I remember the feeling I always get before going on stage. The cringing anxiety and rush of adrenaline are always a pain to deal with. It's the same feeling you get before running a race or getting into a fight. Even so, I already felt like a winner. The fact that I had busked and practiced mercilessly on end just to be there gave me power. I felt in control of myself and of the circumstances. I was happy with the performance I gave, but even more so when they announced my name at the awards ceremony,

"1st prize goes to Ryan Howland!"

The words echoed through my head for days. It was at that very moment that I realized I might actually have it in me to become great violin player. I had taken a big step forward towards reaching my goals and had also gained a tremendous amount of much needed confidence. When I arrived back home, the first thing my mother told me was,

"See? I told you the busking was worth it!"

CHAPTER

Busking

OVER THE YEARS, busking has been one of my most reliable resources. Ever since I started playing the violin at age 5, I would busk every summer with my brother in the streets of downtown Victoria BC. The first pieces we played were from the Suzuki method like Twinkle, Twinkle, Little Star by Mozart. Nowadays, I would stroll down the street, whip out my fiddle and blast out show pieces like Niccolò Paganini's 24 Caprices and the Sonatas and Partitas by Johann Sebastian Bach. Pieces like Meditation from Thais and Air on the G String were of course especially adored by the public. In return, people would toss a few coins into my case and in rare cases, as much as one or two hundred dollars from a single person.

Like everything else, busking started out as just another random hobby of mine. However, between the ages of 13 and 16, it had ultimately become my part-time job, as that was when my study costs were starting to get high. As I gradually started to get better at the violin, I eventually started traveling back and forth from Canada and Switzerland to take masterclasses with professor Bron and his assistant Maurizio Sciarretta. Thanks to their fantastic tuition and my hard work, I was improving rapidly and learning so much. But of course, the price to pay for that was a lot. It was as if the better I got, the more money we would have to pay. As I did not come from a wealthy family, it was an extremely difficult task. The only solution was to get the funds myself through busking. For years, I would take my lessons in Europe, then fly back to Canada for a few months to busk again in order to pay for my next trip. I busked every day for hours on top of my regular practice schedule. It was tedious and painful work, but it was necessary and I was determined to make my studies possible.

As a classical music busker, I was quite the attraction. Most people are not used to such direct exposure to classical music; it took them by surprise and left them in wonder. One of my most favorite things to do while busking is observing the reactions the people walking by. I would always wonder which pieces are the most interesting and relatable to the general public. For example, when playing slow and lyrical pieces with only a single line and no harmony, more people seem to take interest. That is probably because people who are casually walking by only want to hear something simple and beautiful that they can understand right away. To my surprise, my least successful pieces were the most technically demanding ones, specifically the Paganini Caprices. Even if I played like a real virtuoso, nobody seemed to understand violin technique and were instead more attracted to the simple and more musical pieces. Unfortunately for me, it's the weirdest feeling to play the hardest piece for violin only to have zero reaction from the public, whereas when I play the easiest piece like Meditation from Thais, everyone gathers around and claps frantically. My many years of busking have not only supported my tuition fees, but have also taught me a lot about performing and life in general. I have come across many amazing stories and encounters that I am sure I will tell for the rest of my life.

Musical Impact

One day, my mother was sitting nearby watching me busk as usual. Many spectators came and went, throwing in a few coins every so often. I played through some pieces by Bach and Paganini, just like any other day. I never would have guessed that that particular day would forever change my views on music.

A man, who seemed nothing out of the ordinary, sat down beside my mother. As my mother was very talkative, she and the man began to casually converse all the while listening to me busk. He revealed that he was from Scotland and was heavily entranced my music. The two of them talked for a while about life in general and how beautiful the sound of my violin was. But it was as soon as I decided to play the Meditation from Thais that the whole situation changed. It was one of my best pieces and I always wait for the right moment to play it. A few seconds later, the Scottish man lost his words immediately and suddenly looked as if something was stuck in his throat. Strangely enough, the man started to cry. My mother was confused and didn't know how to react. But before she could even say anything, he stood up and quickly walked away. My mother went off after him, curious and sympathetic. Even though he was a stranger, she was worried. She caught up to him and kindly asked if he was okay. He promptly replied that he was fine then quickly left once again. That was that, we thought. We were left in bewilderment by this mysterious person who we were sure we would never see again.

To our surprise, the Scottish man came again the very next day. I was busking at the same place at approximately the same time. My mother asked him once again if he was alright and he apologetically said he was fine. He then explained to her how my music had penetrated his inner feelings and brought him to remember his past, resultantly spilling his emotions.

"Not many people can play classical music like this nowadays," he said.

Although he did not want to say exactly what had happened to him, he admitted that something about my violin playing strummed deeply at his heartstrings. It was an experience that I will never forget.

Through my part-time job of busking on the street, I was able to witness such a remarkable event. It was because of my music that this man revealed his hidden feelings on such a deep level of emotion to the point where he was reminded of the sorrow he held in his heart. It was the first time I realized the true meaning of music and my potential to bring it out to the surface.

Busking in the Cold

Even though I relied on busking, it was not something I particularly enjoyed doing. The main reason being that outdoor conditions can make it extremely difficult and frustrating to play. Furthermore, I had so much pressure from payment deadlines and upcoming trips to Europe that I couldn't afford to take any days off. Even on cold winter days when the temperature dropped close to 0 degrees, I would bare the frustration and force my hands to keep on moving. I had some opened fingered gloves to help keep my hands warm, but I had to rely mostly on my own persistence. Sometimes, my finger joints would be so cold that it would be impossible to make a decent sound. Every slight movement was just unbearable. When I busked with my brother, we had to carry a heavy stand and bring several clips to keep our music scores from blowing away. Sometimes it would be so windy that the whole stand would blow over. When it rained, I could only hope that the overhead rise above me would protect my violin. If I couldn't deal with the weather, I would never be able to raise enough money for my studies. It was yet another sacrifice that I was forced to deal with.

One night, another violin student who was also busking nearby came up to me and asked,

"How can you still play in tune? It's so cold!"

My reply shocked him. I said,

"It's all mental, you just have to adapt to the conditions."

After playing so much in the cold, I gradually stopped feeling the numbness in my hands.

When it came to the instrument itself, I was taking a huge risk. A violin could easily be damaged when exposed to such extreme weather. Especially since I was playing on a 300 year old violin previously used by violinist Eugene Fodor, it was almost too risky. I didn't bring my good bow out into the cold, but I didn't have a choice with my violin as that was the only one I had. Luckily, the consequences were minimal as I only had to get two open seams on the sides of the violin glued back together at the local luthier. It could have been a lot worse. When I would sometimes lose motivation to busk as I was worried about my violin, my mother would always be there to remind me of why I was doing it. It was a risk I would have to take. If I wanted to reach my goals, I would have to keep busking. During these cold days, I reminded myself over and over again that I would only reach success if I kept on pushing through when most people would give up.

Schindler's List

The Theme from Schindler's List is one of my favorite pieces of music. Composed by John Williams, this piece was featured as the main theme of the movie Schindler's List from 1993, covering the sad and tragic history of the holocaust during World War II. Whenever I play this piece on the street, I am always on alert to see if anyone recognizes the famous melody and historical meaning that it portrays.

One day, an old Jewish man came to watch my busking performance. He sat down nearby and listened patiently with a seemingly intense concentration as I played the theme from Schindler's List. From his appearance, I had a feeling that he might be of Jewish decent. After playing a few more pieces, he eventually approached me and asked if I could play the theme from Schindler's List again and of course, I agreed. It was at that moment that I realized he was definitely Jewish, judging by the way he comported himself. I was mostly guessing at the time based off of prior experience, but I later learned that my instincts were indeed correct. The Jewish man began visiting me almost every day after that. Each time, he listened with the same profoundness, as if deep in thought. He would ask me to play the Schindler's List every time he saw me. I was pleased to play it however many times he wanted, but I would always wonder why exactly he was so attached to it. Eventually, he decided to strike up a conversation with my mother and me.

"I pass by this area quite often and not many people can play classical music like you do. Most of the time it's all bad music."

The Jewish man then told us a little bit about his past. When he was just 2 years old, his parents sent him away from Israel to Russia because of the war outbreak. He grew up in Russia, but he never saw his father again. He explained how this piece reminded him of when he was young and of the hardships he was forced to go through because of the war.

"It's a very touching piece, especially for me," he said "...and you play it beautifully."

I was yet again astonished by the capability of music and its relation to the people of the world. I never would have known or felt such a connection to the tragic past of the holocaust if not for the music that brought me closer to it.

Generous Passers-by

There are many things I never would have acknowledged or appreciated if not for busking. Although it was a strenuous and painful job, I have never regretted any of it as it has taught me so much about the meaning of music and how influential it can be. I even made a few friends with the local homeless people who would listen to me all day long. It was a unique experience for me to be so close to these people and to learn of how life could be cruel to them. When my mother was a student 20 years ago, she would always see one peculiar man who would roam the streets completely drunk. Today, he sits in a wheelchair, paralyzed and unable to speak clearly. Often times, these poor people would come up to me and drop their little reserves of money left into my case, when they clearly needed it more themselves. Things like those are always beating at the back of my mind, particularly when I can relate to a certain degree. I feel like one day, I want give back to the people who have helped me on my journey. So far, I have received so much support. One day, I will return it all.

CHAPTER 8

My Sacrifice

A S SOON AS I began my daily 8 hour practice regimen, it was the only thing I could think about. I started to live every day of my life with only one thing on my mind: to practice and improve. I had to sacrifice practically everything else I used to do in my daily life. As I mentioned before, the first thing I gave up was school. I took a whole year off as I felt I needed to improve more than anything else at the time. My mother was not against my decision as she always saw how tired and exhausted I looked after practicing heaps of hours into the night. She trusted my decision and also disliked the fact that I sometimes had to practice until 1 or 2 in the morning. I was determined beyond belief to improve and I knew this was the only way to become the violinist that I wanted to be. Aside from school, I also gave up playing tennis. Although I loved playing tennis competitively, my passion for the violin got so great that I did not hesitate to put it down. If I could get one step closer to my goals, I was happy.

I would stay indoors practicing for almost the whole day without going out or talking to anyone. I distanced myself from my friends and the outside world. When my friends invited me out to parties, I promptly declined, saying that I had to practice instead. I was no longer an ordinary teenager. A lot kids my age spend their days going out with their friends, partying and playing video games without any direction in life. However, my mindset had completely grown out of that.

After one whole year of practicing 8 hours a day, I finally began to calm down. Nowadays, I am practicing slightly less in order to accommodate more time every day to relax, go out and live a social life. I am continuing school online because I know it is important and I also need to save as much time as possible to practice. I was prepared from the beginning to accept these sacrifices; they are absolutely necessary if I wish to become a world class violinist. That is the foremost reason for my willingness to sacrifice so much.

CHAPTER

Contradicting Opinions – Part 1

AS ONE COULD imagine, not everybody approves of my decision to follow the lonely and disciplined path to becoming a world famous violinist. Ever since I made up my mind to pursue music to such a high level, I have been faced with just as much criticism and uncertainties as positive support. For instance, some of my biggest supporters are my mother and her family in Taiwan. When they see my hard work and determination, they are pleased to help me without a second thought. They have even aided me financially on many occasions, which I appreciate enormously. On the other hand, there are many others that I cannot say the same about. I can recall numerous situations in the past few years when I have been confronted with disapproval from close friends and family, questioning my decisions and the path I have decided to follow. I constantly hear things like "Are you really that good at violin?" or "Is it really worth it to try so hard?" Some of our closest friends have even turned their backs on us and run away from what seems to be a deluded violinist and an over supportive mother. I have even asked myself these questions several times, consumed by the negativity. However, I have enough wits to know what I should listen to and what would instead lead me astray. Even then, the judgments continue to pester me.

My father and many others believe that it is best for me to remain in Canada to complete my regular schooling as well as my musical education. In a sense, they are not wrong. Following their advice would probably lead me to being a good musician and most people would be satisfied with that. However, I am looking at a much bigger picture. I want to become something that I never would be by staying in the comfort of my home. To climb to the top of the music world, I will have to follow a very specific and personal path that I would not find in Canada. Supposedly, pursuing music to such a degree is just too difficult for some to believe in. Even now, as I have come so far in my violin playing and am advancing rapidly, the criticism will most likely never end. With that in mind, doubting myself is out of the question at this point in time as my mind is already made.

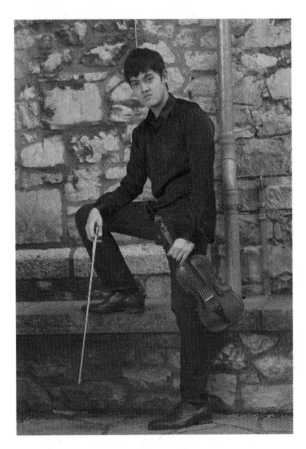

CHAPTER *10*

Contradicting Opinions – Part 2

WHEN I WAS 14, I received a lucky opportunity to study with professor Bron's assistant, Maurizio Sciarretta, in Italy. It had been suggested to us during a previous masterclass, while my mother was talking to him about where the best place to study music is. The news was extremely exciting. After some planning, we decided I would go to Italy by myself for two weeks in the spring. Maurizio was even willing enough to let me stay with him in his family's big house. This would be an amazing opportunity to improve and I knew there was a lot I could learn from Maurizio. The trip was all planned out and I was ready to go, if not for one last problem. Although my mother supported the trip, my father wasn't completely convinced. I remember having a long talk with him in the car a few weeks prior to the trip. He believed that there wasn't much point in going all the way to Italy just to study violin for two weeks, and instead insisted that I stay and carry on with my normal life at home. It would be an expensive trip and I suppose he disliked that fact. But aside from that, there wasn't much else supporting his opinion. It also made me uncomfortable. I had just reached the surface only to be immediately pulled back down. It took a while, but I was finally able to convince my father to let me go. Young people need exposure, especially around the delicate ages of 14 or 15, in order to grow and discover new things for themselves. That's why I just wouldn't give up on the opportunity at hand as I knew it would be one of the most influential ones yet. As it turned out, I was exactly right. Those two weeks in Italy ending up being one some of the most important experiences that I would be lucky enough to come across in my whole life. My teacher taught me many important musical ideas and fundamentals to violin playing that I will forever rely on as a base to my technique; Maurizio drilled them into my bones. Aside from the violin, I also got to experience a whole new culture by living with Italians. I think a lot of people nowadays underestimate just how much one can develop by being exposed to new worlds and ideas. I can confidently say the trip changed my whole perspective. In addition, those two weeks opened up several new opportunities to come back time and time again. Since then, I have visited Italy multiple times to study with Maurizio, to meet new people and to perform for new audiences. When I think back to the first time my father disagreed, it would have been a shame if I had listened.

Standing beside my 198 cm tall teacher Maurizio Sciarretta

CHAPTER  11

The World

PURSUING MUSIC HAS given me countless opportunities to travel all over the globe for lessons and masterclasses. However, the beginning of my passions and aspirations trace back to the early ages of my childhood. Ever since my mind's eye was exposed to the various influential cultures of the world, I have observed and absorbed the antiquities of civilization which have all helped develop my personality of today. I was younger than 4 when I first breathed in the eastern air of my second homeland, Taiwan. Yet it was at age 7 that I lay before the tall looming churches of the vibrant European culture during my first trip to Europe.

We spent several months of planning and almost a year of saving up the funds for what would be the first eye-opening experience in my life. As my mother was an extremely considerate parent, she didn't want my brother and me to be stuck in one place. During this trip, we would see 33 concerts in the 39 days that we would be visiting Europe. My brother was 10 and I was only 7 as we were empowered by the many symphony concerts, operas, ballets, theatrical plays, museums and historical sites that we were fortunate enough to witness.

For a child, such unique opportunities can be extremely influential. Despite my young age, I still remember staring down at Mozart's own violin in Salzburg, Austria, and the eerie sensation that if I were to peel my eyes away ever so slightly, the glistening piece of art would disappear. In Auswitch, I stood before the countless glass encasements of shoes, bags and hair that belonged to the prisoners of the concentration camp. The moment you walk into such a place, all hairs stand on end. The tension was real and the memory is nearly fresh in my head.

To be in Europe is like being at the heart of the music world. That was where many of history's most contributing classical music personalities came from. As a young musician, I was very lucky to have been introduced to such a broad new prospective. To imagine that I went all the way from Canada to the Franz Liszt and Frédéric Chopin houses as well as almost every major city in Europe is incredible.

CHAPTER  12

Five Competitions in One Year

A T THE AGE of 15, I made a solemn decision. I wanted my 15th year to be the last year I spent catching up to the amazing players I idolized. I wanted to improve past the limitations of an average player and begin my true journey as a young professional. I was ready to do anything to make that happen and I knew the best way to accomplish that was to participate in competitions.

Even though most teacher's recommend participating in only one or two competitions per year, I wanted to push myself much farther. I planned out the whole year with 5 big international competitions. I didn't ask for anybody's approval as I knew they would just think I was overwhelming myself. I only wanted to improve, and I hoped this challenge would allow me to attain new skills and more performance experience. During that year, I had to prepare loads of difficult repertoire and practice countless hours to get my level of playing as close to perfection as possible. I focused to a great extent of dedication and payed much more attention to the details of my playing than ever before. I was in need of a boost, and luckily I got just that.

The first of the five competitions I attended was in Bern, Switzerland, and it was huge. I had 4 months to prepare for it and considering the enormous amount of extremely difficult repertoire there was, I was almost discouraged. I was about to venture into a whole new world of music, where the level of playing was unbelievably higher than mine. It felt as if I were a big fish from a small pond being poured into the ocean. Even so, I didn't back out. Only a handful of violinists in the world would be capable of playing the required pieces such as the Paganini Caprice no. 4 and Bloch Sonata no. 1, and I wanted to be a part of that handful. I knew that my skill level at the time was years away from attempting such a challenge, but I also had faith in my ability to learn new techniques quickly. After a lot of strenuous practicing, I managed to prepare the pieces just in time for the competition. Thinking back at the experience, I realize just how crazy I was. I competed against world-class players up to the age of 30 and among the jury members were some of the biggest and most famed personalities in the world. In the end, I didn't win any prizes, but I played well and was satisfied with the result of my progress, fulfilling my intended goal.

Just two months later, I went to Belgium for my next competition. Like before, I planned out my practice routine in order to quickly master all of the pieces that I would be playing. The pieces I chose this time were more musically profound as well as technically difficult such as the Bach Chaconne and again the fiendishly difficult Paganini Caprice no. 4. Luckily, I has studied my new repertoire with professor Bron and his assistant, so I was well prepared and knew I would make a big impression as a 15 year old. After the competition, I received many complements from the jury members for my remarkable performance and stimulating musical ideas. I made it to the finals, but didn't win. Nevertheless, it was probably one of my most favorite competition experiences as it gave me more confidence as a performer as well as the opportunity to perform in a wonderful concert hall.

Two more competitions past until my last one finally came in Bucharest, Romania. Only this time, I had a lot more riding on my shoulders. As our financial situation was getting tight, I had to rely mostly on the support from friends and family who believed in my potential and knew just how much I could improve from going to the competition.

Three weeks prior to the first round, I practiced 10 hours a day. Because of the sacrifices my supporters had to make, I felt as if I really needed to win in order to not let them down. All day and all night, I practiced to perfection. All the while, I carried a nauseating feeling in my gut. The fear of failing everyone who believed in me ate away at my insides. Even though I was ready to play my best, thanks to the countless hours of practice, I couldn't shake the pressure. My mother and I were running so low on money that I began to believe that if I did not win the competition prize money, I would not be able to pay for my lessons nor for food to survive. The night before the first round, a voice echoed in my head,

"You have to win!"
"You'll have no money left to survive if you lose!"

The reality was just as bad as the voices told me and I knew it all too well. I went up on stage and gave a poor and nervous performance- hands and body shaking all over. As soon as I played the first few notes, I knew that I had failed to overcome the stress. It was even more frustrating when I realized that even after practicing 10 hours every day, it didn't make a difference as the pressure took it all away. I was shocked. I felt like no matter how hard I worked, none of it mattered if I couldn't overcome the direness of the situation. Even today, I am still trying to figure out how to clear my mind, despite my hardships. After the competition, we were lucky enough to have our friends support us for a little bit longer. Thanks to that, I was able to pull myself back together and go home to start practicing again.

CHAPTER  13

Continuous Struggles

I CANNOT IMAGINE A more difficult time in my life so far than right now. Ever since I became so fanatical about the violin, things have gotten extremely difficult emotionally and financially. From age 14, almost all of the costs of my studies and travels have been funded by busking and support from the public, friends and family. Because my mother has been a single parent since I was 2, it was never easy, especially since my brother and I had such big ambitions. There have been so many times in the past when we literally had zero money left to survive. I am never satisfied with my current level of playing and I can't let financial barriers prevent me from improving.

To study music at a world class level is indeed very expensive. Other fields like sports and academics are the same. It just depends on how far one wishes to go. My brother is almost as hardworking as myself and is studying art and animation in Paris, France. Even though we may have the capability, the passion, and the hard work, the only thing that is missing is our financial stability, which we often cannot control.

Many of our friends who have been supporting the three of us seem to eventually drift away, not wanting to get involved in our huge ambitions. It seems hard for people to understand that my brother and I do not want to be stationed in one place, unable to reach out to the future. I think many musicians also struggle with the problem of support nowadays. I wish to pursue music, but not just casually in my hometown in Canada.

My standards are much higher than that. Without pushing everything to the highest degree, I would never be able to reach my goals. Ambition without money is terribly difficult. The only thing we are rich in is soul and the will to continue striving.

CHAPTER

Parent's Sacrifice

SACRIFICE FROM PARENTS is absolutely essential when determining the height of their children's lives. I was fortunate to have plenty of support from my parents as a child.

My mother lived with her older siblings when she was growing up in Taiwan as her parents were never around. But it is because her childhood was so lacking of proper parental care that she has become so considerate today. As a parent, she wanted to give my brother and me the things she never received herself. She even treated her students with the same generosity. She would do things like pick them up and take them to and from lessons and she would always drive home the last student of the day. Often times, she would even prepare food and snacks for them. On student's birthdays, she would bake homemade cakes to surprise them as they arrived for their lesson. The atmosphere she created in her home studio was unlike any other in the whole world. You would never find another serious music teacher who would treat their students with the same manner.

My mother does not believe in giving up due to financial barriers. Often times, she would ask friends and family for support and ask students to make early payments when my brother and I had opportunities to take extensive classes and programs. Her student's parents knew that my brother and I had a lot of potential and didn't hesitate pay her early.

Another part of my mother's nature is the gift of giving. She is the complete opposite of materialistic and doesn't mind letting go of things for the benefit of others. In Chinese culture, people strongly believe that if you do good things, good things will come back to you- those are the exact words that my mother constantly reminds me of. I have been given so much in my life just for sake of making my future career. Sometimes, I feel spoiled even though I know there is no other way to reach the top. Without endless amounts of help, it would be impossible. That is why I always try to give back to the people of the world in any way possible, whether it may be in the form of music or even something entirely different.

My father is almost the complete opposite of my mother. Like a mathematician, he often conducts himself with a very clear and straightforward manner. When making decisions, he looks mainly at the facts in order to decide rationally, whilst my mother makes her decisions mostly based on feeling. A balance of both is probably the best.

When I was small, my father would often take my brother and me to see symphony concerts and operas. He exposed us to the world with a different quality as mother was always too busy to take us out. After concerts, my brother and I would wait backstage for him to come out and greet us. I always thought it made us cool to have easy backstage access after concerts. As ambitious as I was, it was just as important to relax. Watching movies, hiking in the woods, fishing and eating Subway helped me keep positive childhood memories. Nearly every Christmas, he would take us to visit my grandparents and his side of the family in Kamloops BC. It was a long 8 hour road trip to make and some of my fondest memories were made there.

Catching loads of fish with my dad and brother

CHAPTER

Mother's story – part 1

PROBABLY THE MOST interesting person I have ever known is none other than my mother. The number of unbelievable stories and hardships she has gone through have drastically effected my own life and where I am today. As life can be unpredictable at times, we have made many mistakes and faced a lot of disappointment. But even so, we don't regret any of it because there is no such thing as a smooth road to success.

My mother chose to devote the majority of her life to supporting my brother and me and she lived sully or that purpose. Incidentally, her whole life of only playing the piano made her a little bit naïve. She was always too kind and believing and didn't know of the hardships and betrayal that life can bring. That was her weakness.

Because my mother was so nice to the people around her, she was often taken for granted. My brother and I are partly to blame simply from having so much ambition. Many of my mother's friends, boyfriends and supporters have run away after learning that she was alone to support two unbelievably hardworking sons with such incredibly high goals. Before long, a lot of people had already left her. Maybe it was because they were jealous of the fact that we can try so hard and achieve so much without fearing failure. But what they don't see are the mistakes we've made and the obstacles we've had to overcome in order to be where we are right now.

When I was 14 years old, my mother fiancé proposed that she and I move to Europe together to live with him. After a lot of thought, we decided it would be a golden opportunity as I would finally be able to be close to my teachers instead of flying back and forth between Canada and Switzerland every few months. Thus, we packed all of our bags and put the house up on sale in preparation to move to Europe. My brother and I were just starting to get closer to our goals and the extra push would help us reach even greater heights. As hopeful as my mother was, she believed it would all turn out well. The only problem was her fiancé's lack of conviction.

After finally installing ourselves into our new home, my mother's relationship took a turn for the worst. The man she had thought to be a caring and honest person had turned into a monster in as little as a week. His behavior had completely changed to the point where he began spitting insults and verbal abuse at her for days on end. All I could do was stand there and watch. At first, we didn't understand. How could he have changed so fast? Why was he no longer the kind and considerate person he was before? He had known my mother for a long time and they knew each other well; he had already proven himself to be a good person. It didn't make any sense and it took us a long time to figure out the reason.

The laws of women's protection in Europe are very strict. In most cases, when a married couple divorces, the man is obliged to give up his house as well as half his income to the woman by law. As my mother's fiancé had already divorced once before, he had become scared about having another marriage and resultantly pushed her aside. The consequence was grave. My mother and I had to move back to Canada, where her teaching position at the conservatory and all of her students were already gone. But for her, that wasn't the worst part. What shocked her the most was the fact that she had lost an opportunity for me to finally be able to study music full time in Europe. That guilt threw her into a state of misery.

I was also disappointed in what had happened. We had already given up so much in Canada that I didn't want to go back; I knew our lives would never be the same as before. Our friends and relatives judged my mother harshly for messing up, even though her intentions were truly for the greater good. Very few parents would go through so much for the sake of their children and most wouldn't do anything at all to seize such opportunities. However, I did learn and develop a lot from the experience. With that perspective, nothing is ever wasted. It is better to strive and fail, then to succeed without striving.

Following the events in Europe, my mother and I attempted to find our old lives again. I went back to my regular high school while my mother brought back a few old students, but she mostly had to find new ones. Not even the conservatory wanted to take her back even though she had taught there for 20 years. Because of that, she had to work another job aside from teaching at home.

Under our circumstances and low income, we were only able to survive for half a year before we were forced give up our house. It was an unfortunate fate, but we also saw it as an opportunity to move on with our lives. My mother would rather pay for my brother's studies in Paris and for my musical education than to keep paying for the house. After it was gone, we really didn't have anything left in Canada. It was a painful loss, especially since I had only just turned 15. I never thought life could be so cruel. It left a hole in my heart.

in front our house in Victoria, BC

CHAPTER 16

A New beginning

OUR STAY WITH my mother's former fiancé did have it merits. In fact, our short time of living in Europe brought me to meet my next teacher, Rudolf Koelman, a former pupil of the legendary violinist, Jascha Heifetz.

I discovered the violinist while casually browsing YouTube one day. The first recording I heard of him was the piece I was studying at the time- Caprice no. 16 by Paganini. After listening to the first few bars, I could tell whoever was playing knew what they were doing. But it was after listening to his performances of virtuoso pieces like Tzigane by Ravel and Zigeunerweisen by Sarasate that I really became interested in the player's style. His tone was harsh and gritty, yet warm and full of color at the same time, like a coal of hot fire. On top of all that, his sense of virtuosity was incredibly wild. I instantly became obsessed with it. As soon as I read online that Rudolf Koelman was a professor in Zurich, right beside where I was, it was clear what I had to do next. My mother and I sent him a Facebook message asking for a lesson and easily enough, he agreed. The next thing I knew, I was standing outside of professor Koelman's house, eagerly waiting for the clock to strike 10. I was surprised to see him arrive from the distance while casually riding his bicycle as I had never seen a famous musician up close attending their daily lives, they were normal people too. From his appearance, I could tell he was indeed professor Koelman, despite the fact that he looked far too young to be a 56 year old Dutch violinist.

Professor Koelman invited me into his home and I played for him for about an hour and a half. I didn't know what to expect, but I was confident enough in my abilities. He gave me a summary of what he thought of my playing and what we would work on before picking up his violin to demonstrate. Everything was going well so far. Koelman had a great mind for music and technique, I was glad to be there. However, what stunned me the most was the moment he drew his bow across the strings of his violin. An arrangement of sounds and color instantly filled the room to the point where I was in awe. A true soloist was right before me, it was inspirational. The sound he produced was far greater than what I heard in his recordings and the Heifetz-like tone left a permanent impression on me. After the lesson he became my favorite player. I went home dazzled and I instantly knew that I wanted to study with him.

During the last month we had in our house, I was miraculously accepted to study in Zurich, Switzerland with non-other than the maestro Rudolf Koelman. It was ironic how we had just been kicked out of the same place, only to be given the chance to come back one year later. We didn't have a lot of money left over, but we knew it was a chance I couldn't miss out on and we were prepared to make the necessary sacrifices in order to make it happen. In the new semester, I began my studies in Zurich, Switzerland.

With my teacher Rudolf Koelman after our first lesson

CHAPTER  17

Mother's Story - part 2

A T THE SAME time I was accepted to study with Professor Koelman, my mother inevitably found herself in another predicament that was even worse than the last one. She had met yet another man, who was eager to marry her and convince her to live with him in Germany. Although my mother was much more skeptic than before, this man was much nicer and more faithful than the last. He was also very supportive of our goals and he even helped us out financially on many occasions.

Since my mother's last experience in Europe, I was much less trusting. Even though I wished for the best, the last thing I wanted was for the same tragedy to repeat itself again. Eventually, time made me believe that this man was much better than the last and the doubt I had left in me was little to none. For the most part, I was right. However, the past few years have taught me that one can never truly see nor understand every corner of someone. And of course, my mother's German fiancé finally revealed his hidden colors, just as she was about to move in with him in Germany.

It was a mixture of bad luck and unforeseen circumstances that things didn't work out as intended. The German man's plan was to divorce his current wife and have my mother move in afterwards. Unfortunately, it wasn't that simple. He most likely didn't think ahead far enough and failed to consider that if he were to divorce his wife, he would end up losing his house to her. Caught up in the stress of his situation, he chose material over love. He decided to stay with his old wife, even though he was not happy with their relationship, all because he wanted to keep his house. Despite all the time he had spent with my mother and all the rambling about their future, his house was his true pride and joy in the end. He did not want to lose it for anything, even for my mother whom he had made a serious promise with. The two of them had been through so much already, but it didn't matter to him. He simply left my mother on the streets in the middle of nowhere, in a foreign country completely unknown to her. The worst part was that he didn't even bother helping her find a place to stay. He just dropped everything and left while pushing my mother away at the last possible second.

We couldn't believe it. The German man was also having difficulties with his job at the time, supposedly his decision was influenced by his work. As for my mother, she only became more and more depressed as she knew she couldn't do anything to change the situation. With nowhere to go and no one to help, another miracle turned the tides.

One day, my mother was on the bus trying to figure out the directions to city hall on a map. With little success, a senior man sitting beside her offered to help her out. He introduced himself as Dr. Loschen, a doctor in biology, and kindly guided her to the right destination. He was so kindhearted that he even went in with her to translate the whole appointment from German to English. Afterwards, he offered to help her out with her next errand at the bank. Dr. Loschen helped her fill out paperwork as well as translate appointments. They then went out for lunch and after back to his apartment for tea. Little did my mother know that the fateful encounter with the 72 year old doctor turned out to be one of the biggest miracles in my mother's entire life. It was only a few days after meeting the doctor that she was abandoned by her German fiancé. In distress and confusion, she emailed the old man asking for his advice. He replied,

"Why not stay in my apartment? I have a free room!"

Even though my mother didn't want to rely on the generosity of someone she had just met, she had no other choice. It was an unanticipated twist of fate and it was crazy to think that the man she had run into on the bus ended up being her savior.

The time my mother spent in Dr. Loschen's apartment saved her from absolute despair. Little by little, he would console her and try to cheer her up. After some time, his efforts prevailed. Eventually, my mother started cooking for Dr. Loschen and cleaning his place as thanks. She didn't have any money left so that was the only way she could help him. It was like a two way trust. Dr. Loschen also benefited a lot from having my mother there. He had been living alone for years with only his dog to keep him company. A lot of the time, he didn't eat or take care of himself very well, but my mother helped prevent that. Five months went by in the blink of an eye, until it was my turn to face despair.

CHAPTER *18*

Despair

Finally, after such a long and difficult journey, I had achieved my goal of studying full time with a world renowned teacher in Europe. While my mother was dealing with her problems in Germany, I was living alone right beside professor Koelman's home in Switzerland. Every week, I attended theory classes at the music school and private lessons at my teacher's house. Everything was going well and I was learning so much from professor Koelman. But of course, fate wasn't going to let me study so easily without throwing more problems into my life. After three months of successful studying in Switzerland, my student visa was rejected and I was forced to leave the country. I had already spent far too long waiting to be in a good program with a world renowned teacher, it was too cruel when the opportunity was swiped away from me for no good reason.

When I first began my studies in Switzerland, I was permitted to live there under temporary tourist status while I waited for my student visa to be approved. There shouldn't have been any problems with issuing my visa as we made sure that all of our documents were intact and sufficient. But when it started to take much longer than expected to receive an answer, I was forced to fly out of Switzerland as my tourist visa had expired. Things only got worse from there. The plan was to fly to Taiwan for two weeks where I would stay with my aunt and my cousins while I waited for what seemed to be positive results from the visa office. As I had to renew my violin loan from Taiwan at the same time, it worked out perfectly. At least that's what I thought.

Two weeks turned into a month, then two months and more. I ended up spending the majority of my stay writing emails and getting forms together in order to obtain my visa. My uncle and I even made several trips back and forth from the visa branch in Taiwan to ask questions and to make sure everything would go smoothly. All the while, I was missing all of my lessons and classes that we worked so hard to pay for. It was extremely frustrating. I wanted to get back as soon as possible, but I was trapped, hanging in the air, seething and loathing for the answer. Three months had gone by when I finally received the answer. It was 2:30 am, when my mother called me from Germany. I remember the conversation well. She asked me,

"Will you be disappointed if you don't get your visa?
"No", I lied.
She then said what I feared the most.
"The answer is no, you didn't get it."

My stomach welled up. From that very moment, I felt defeated and utterly useless. Despite all the help and support I received from my family and friends in Taiwan, it still didn't work. After the call, I stood in the middle of my room for what seemed like the whole night, contemplating on what had just happened. I was in absolute disbelief and frustration. I felt as if my whole life was leading up to that moment, only to have it all taken away from me in a matter of seconds. The hardest part from then on would be figuring out what I would do next, how I would find another teacher and whether or not I should just wait one whole year to apply again for the same program. I was already lucky to have met professor Koelman and to think just how long it would take to find another world renowned teacher willing to take me on as a student seemed almost impossible. I wanted to be the best player, but without the best teacher my dreams would end before they even started.

I took my anger out on the countless mosquitos flying around my room. I killed them over and over again with an electric racquet until there were none left. I was infuriated. All those weeks I spent working and hoping were for nothing. It was like climbing out of an abyss only to find nothing above. I thought professor Koelman would be my teacher for many years to come, but I guess I was naïve. I didn't show it on the outside as I never show anything, but I really was struck hard by the turn of events. Ever so slowly, I began to plan what to do next. I flew to Germany to join my mother in Dr. Loschen's apartment and spent the next three months searching new possibilities and looking for a new teacher.

CHAPTER

Best Failure

ONE MONTH AFTER entering Germany, I participated in the same competition in Belgium as I did a year before, only this time I was in the oldest age category. Honestly, I had no expectations in winning or even doing well as I had not had any lessons in over 4 months. All of the other competitors had studied their pieces with their teachers time and time again and knew what they were doing, while I was going just for the sake of playing.

In the first round of the competition, I played works by Eugène Ysaÿe and Niccolò Paganini. As expected, everything went well technically, but my performance lacked musical depth and knowledge. When I asked the jury members about my playing. All of their comments went along the lines of,

"You have so much talent and such amazing hands, but it doesn't seem like you know what you are doing with the music."

Of course, everything made sense to them once I explained how I had learned all of the pieces by myself. That came as a huge shock as nobody else would be as crazy as to participate in such a big competition without proper preparation. One of the jury members told me that I played like a bird flying through the sky with no limits or boundaries, when my music should have been much more refined like a perfectly framed painting or sculpture. In the end, I didn't make it past the first round. Practicing hours on end by myself at home wouldn't be enough to win a competition, much less to reach my goals.

My luck finally started to turn around after one of the most important jury members of the competition, famed violinist and pedagogue Dora Schwarzberg, sat me down for long talk where she revealed all of my faults and weaknesses. Even though she had only heard me play once, she could already see right through me.

"You play as if you don't really care what comes out to the audience. It could be that you love the music so much that you only hear it on the inside and don't know how to communicate it. Like a beautiful baby, where everything is perfect, but the baby doesn't yet know anything about the world. I think you need a teacher," she said with a laugh.

After hearing all of that, I was speechless. Professor Schwarzberg was incredibly knowledgeable. If there was anyone who could help me find a new teacher, it would be her. I only had one teacher in mind whom I wanted to study with and I quickly threw his name out,

"Do you know Viktor Tretyakov?"

Professor Schwarzberg paused for at least ten seconds after hearing the name, as if deep in thought. I bet everything on that very moment to find out whether or not she could get me some connection to this teacher. If not, I would be stuck back at square one. I was surprised when she replied with a simple "yes", but then I realized I shouldn't have been. She and Viktor Tretyakov had studied under the same teacher in Russia, I should've known better. From that point on, my future started to see hope. Professor Schwarzberg's next line stunned me even farther.

"I will call him and tell him about you", she promised.

"Don't worry, I will take care of you."

Professor Schwarzberg's words echoed throughout my head for weeks. I couldn't stop hoping for my future studies and that I would finally reach a new starting point. Eventually, I was able to get in contact with prof. Viktor Tretyakov through professor Schwarzberg's recommendation. In short, I played for him in his house in Bonn, Germany, where I had to walk up a mountain to get to, and I assume he liked my playing as he was willing to accept me as his student. As of the time of publishing this book, I am currently studying with prof. Viktor Tretyakov, who won the prestigious Tchaikovsky Competition at age just 19, as part of a private study program with the Blackmore International Music Academy in Germany.

Conclusion

I**T HAS ONLY** been three years since I started to get serious with the violin and so much has happened since then. I almost can't believable how much I have learned and improved during that time. My journey is still at its beginning and I am sure that there will be many more amazing experiences and failures yet to happen. During these past few years, I have received so much help and support from friends and family, I hope that this book will help show them my appreciation and to encourage them to keep believing in me. Once I reach my goal of becoming a world famous violinist, I will return everything that I have been given. I am also hopeful that my stories may help inspire other teenagers in pursuing their endeavors passionately. Not too long ago, I was not much more than an average boy with little determination to amount to anything. All I needed was the will to make the decision of what I wanted to do for myself. Of course, it was not an easy decision to make and my life has never been the same ever since. However, I can say that it was probably the best decision I have ever made in my life.

Musical Awakening

Ryan Howland

Printed in the United States
By Bookmasters